CW00509349

FRANK'S WING

FRANK'S
WING

POEMS

JACOB McARTHUR MOONEY

Copyright © Jacob McArthur Mooney, 2023

Published by ECW Press
665 Gerrard Street East
Toronto, Ontario, Canada M4M 1Y2
416-694-3348 / info@ecwpress.com

All rights reserved. No part of this publication may be
reproduced, stored in a retrieval system, or transmitted
in any form by any process — electronic, mechanical,
photocopying, recording, or otherwise — without the
prior written permission of the copyright owners and
ECW Press. The scanning, uploading, and distribution of
this book via the Internet or via any other means without
the permission of the publisher is illegal and punishable
by law. Please purchase only authorized electronic
editions, and do not participate in or encourage electronic
piracy of copyrighted materials. Your support of the
author's rights is appreciated.

Editor for the Press: Michael Holmes /
a misFit Book
Copy-editor: Emily Schultz

 Cover design: Jessica Albert
Author photo: Elyse Friedman

LIBRARY AND ARCHIVES CANADA CATALOGUING
IN PUBLICATION

Title: Frank's wing : poems / Jacob McArthur Mooney.

Names: Mooney, Jacob McArthur, author.

Identifiers: Canadiana (print) 20220477302 |
Canadiana (ebook) 20220477450

ISBN 978-1-77041-719-9 (softcover)
ISBN 978-1-77852-128-7 (Kindle)
ISBN 978-1-77852-126-3 (ePub)
ISBN 978-1-77852-127-0 (PDF)

Classification: LCC PS8626.O5928 F73 2023 | DDC
C811/.6—dc23

We acknowledge the support of the Canada Council for the Arts. *Nous remercions le Conseil des arts du Canada de son
soutien.* This book is funded in part by the Government of Canada. *Ce livre est financé en partie par le gouvernement du
Canada.* We acknowledge the funding support of the Ontario Arts Council (OAC), an agency of the Government of
Ontario. We also acknowledge the support of the Government of Ontario through the Ontario Book Publishing Tax
Credit, and through Ontario Creates.

"The city is beauty, unbreakable and amorous as eyelids." —Dionne Brand, from *Thirsty*, engraved on paving stone, Schumpeter Park, in 2016

"It's hard to imagine a more intimate relationship between city and citizen. Frank flourished in Toronto, made his fortune there and appeared in three decades of Canada Day parades. His art collection of course outlives him but so do his more typical investments. There is one cold pocket of the earth where the name Schumpeter imagines not dotcom billionaires but buildings: hard, ugly buildings and the hard, ugly city built around them. The Schumpeter Wing isn't reputation laundering, and it's not a change of heart. It's a building, first and foremost, one last ugly building." —*Architecturally Speaking*, CBC Radio 2, 2016

"An interviewer told me, before we started, that I'd need to come clean about which pieces in the gallery were finds and which were reconstructions. I might've convinced him that no one had ever asked me that before." —Frank Schumpeter, 2016

Alta Vistae

*

Reconstruction Efforts

Alta Vista

A blush of fortune flared our city's surfaces.

Joseph Schumpeter, man of Harvard,
had himself three goals: to be Vienna's foremost lover,
Austria's best horseman, and the last economist

the world understood. His only child, Frank—
born Franz after the emperor the family called uncle—
raised the building I was born in. Alta Vista Tower

poked over the Spadina Expressway, near Eglinton,
in 1983. Joseph birthed the term *creative destruction*
and all the smashing magnates it recast as makers.

Maker Frank sowed the sprawl behind
the dagger-bland highway he lobbied into life
to cart our boomers home from whoop and finance.

With his inherited publishing money and charm
Joseph's one surviving son got to sweetening our exits
with garden lots and parking.

Paid a dollar per excavated acre, we heard,
set to tearing up the bungalows of midtown.
One hundred new constructions:

Meidling, Schumpetertown, and then, Alta Vista,
its ribbons of concrete with his bust above the door.
Joseph liked to say he made good

on two of his ambitions, but he wouldn't say which.
Frank had his own. To be his second city's richest man,
to buy his beloved Leafs and win a Cup,

and to grow the greatest art array in all of dour Canada.
He died with no rings but two billions.
Revealed on his deathbed a donation to the gallery

of lost privacies that pinked the board's complexions.
The new wing would restore the building.
A park in his name along the grange.

A quiet man but quick to fight,
Frank took out a policy of beauty
for the city *Forbes* had called:

"the developed world's ugliest,
a six-lane freeway surrounded by snow
and British pessimisms."

Alta Vista aged, gave its name
to Schumpeterian study groups and a search engine.
Steve Wozniak's dog and Peter Thiel's plane.

And was home, too, to the neighbourhood kids
I knew growing up. Latchkey accelerations
of their parents' fiscal limits. Liberal arts

astonishment-seekers gone essentialist
by middle age. Like me, I'm middle-aged.
Like them, I've got opinions about art.

Triptych of the Lost Kandinskys

"If not destroyed after the Nazis' Degenerate Art Expo, the three Kandinskys would have entered the public domain in 1991, and perhaps adorned our common objects: phonebooks, calendars, T-shirts . . ." —Frank Schumpeter

Composition 1 (Phonebook)

There'll be no hope for recognition here.

Don't be embarrassed;
I'm also lost.

I made Frank and all this seeing up to sell a bill of story.

How would you decode these spiritual demands
except to say *I know* and maybe *Thank you?*

In this room there are the books I'll never read
and the books I'll never reread
and then there is the telephone book,
        my other friend.
Though it's not coming with us on the trip.

        It is 1991.
Kandinsky's anchored thoughts
split a dozen cryptic figures
posed in front of one another
to mock us with their pattern,

3

locking arms to necks,
framed but unspoken-of
by Bell's palatial blue.

A clutch of Delta tickets. A nest of Old Milwaukees.
My hand, and the shadow of my hand, and the listings.

Spiritual like the way
an explosively hated idea
          particulates the air
until it settles on new pages.
Spiritual like the non-possession of a body.
Weightless so it falls into its gist,
          into capital.

Adoption. Purchase. Degenerate. "*The.*
Sun. Melts. All. Of. Moscow. Down. To.
A. Single. Spot. Of. Light." Liles. Lillard. Linares.
Lindbergh. Lindbergh. Lindbergh's Pizzeria . . .

Composition II (Calendar)

Highlighter alights on a long weekend:
    Fuck-It Festival
tattooed across the lines meaning
Friday and Saturday nights.

The seasonal relief is all sunspots and dust.
Kandinsky did not love the weather,
but he loved the lidded touch discovered by lit things.
    The words *Terry's Esso*
interrupt his leftmost strokes. Terry exists,
though you have never met him. Still,

it is bourgeois to see a human figure
where there isn't one.

I don't know what Kandinsky meant
when he called himself a prophet.

He died like other people,
which is to say, surprised.

Composition III (T-shirt)

First a novelty tote bag with a picture of the Duke Boys
and a caption joking *Sons of the New South*,
then a kid in a racially insensitive baseball cap,
his dad with Kandinsky's third attempt
stretched from shoulder to *Simpsons* buckle.

The *Fuck-It Festival* flukes towards its lame-duck period
as the temperature slugs to three digits
and a pocket radio plays Whitney Houston
to help the crowds outside Space Mountain
manage their mortality, converting hung terror
into spontaneous Super Bowl pre-games,
the National Waltz into 4/4 time.

The Soviets have given up.
Everyone is digging for oil in the Arctic.
What is one more attempt to explain yourself
as the half-swallowed consequence of art?
I don't know how I got here.
I should be nine years old and sober.
          Florida is golf courses,
gift shops full of bamboo pants.

The dad in the Kandinsky shirt smacks the kid's hat.
It lands face down at my feet saying *Starter*.
          O, public market,
just please don't let me die during wartime.

Loss Rate

The doctor returns
to find me pawing buttons, says
I'm afraid you won't live long enough
to see every piece of art.

His forecast matches my behaviour.
The nurse's station holds watch
in case I try to book it. Back home,
the unopened novels
knock heads together
in the corner of shelves
cladded over with Sprite cans.
A week of kids' videos and lip syncs
siphon through the internet
each second.
                 The analysis of photos,
and the analysis of the faces observing those photos,
won't be recorded for the pleasure
of we who came upon them
in the waiting room magazine's underwear ad.
                 I'll live.
But given the prognosis,
and the patterns of forgetting
that mark my male line's later years,
there will need to be a game of letting go.
Yard sales. Mentorship.
Multi-volume histories
I bought because of cover art
left by fountains or in food courts.
Don't be disappointed,
the doctor encourages.

Art is not for looking at.
Art harangues. It taunts plans.

Portrait of Winston Churchill

Imagine for a minute that you are a public person.
Your voice is always heard. You're always
going to the toilet with your microphone hot.
The nape of your neck is chafed from gaffer tape.
A friend from college grew a beard and rotten politics
and is blogging down your name.
Sports fans trouble you with hisses
when your face invades their jumbotrons.
Your nervous tics are grist for public torment.
Whole briefs on the way you take your tea,
how you hold your wife's hand to cross the street.
You thought you had religion but you were the religion.
Imagine, your surname is an enclave. Your smirk
is an enchantment. Your children were raised
by lecture-light and cameras, and the glut of topicality
their genetics ideate. Your losses are a narrative.
Your wins are a stake. Not dance but kinesics.
Not the meaning of your words,
but the shapes they give your face.

The Day the Clown Cried

"The comedian Harry Shearer was said to comment upon leaving the private showing at Jerry Lewis's house: 'This was a perfect object. This movie is so drastically wrong, its pathos and its comedy are so wildly misplaced, that you could not, in your fantasy of what it might be like, improve on what it really is.'"—Frank Schumpeter

I went to dog-whistle,
but all the dogs arrived
with subpoenas in their jaws,
quivers full of arrows,
and God complexes.
When I held them down
they barked the names of saints.

The cleaner I hired
has stacked my trash like sculpture.
Hold fast: my malignant mouth
will censor every compliment.
Unless I am threatening
to harm myself or others,
come be a made-up mind for me.

Go home, lightweight. Go inefficiently.
Heap my private entrance up with letters.
I'm a soft puncher.
I misplace my feet.
But until I turn a corner
and the corner self-corrects,
know that I'll come back.

Like whichever Greek hero
you feel needs the boost
of this exposure most,
I will come back
like he came back:
a perfect object,
makeup ladies trailing
behind me like a wake.

Planned Descent into a Super Bowl
(In memory of James "Fan Man" Miller)

"They dated Mr. Miller's death to 2002, nine years after he dropped in on Holyfield and Bowe, but admit it could have been earlier depending on conditions." —Frank Schumpeter

The black bear and the brown bear
will come and cut me down,
will take my ropes for bedding,
and break my face.
My son will grow up
to not see himself in me,
will chalk his thick jaw
up to frowning
(the Alaskan coastline
will observe this parenthetically:
a long curve of pack-ice, beached).

A seated silence for my seconds
of recoil and drift, then
I became Electric Man,
a fallen figure. First evidence
of rabble sound was like
a distant river, or the reindeer
now sniffing at my feet.
I circled Caesars Palace,
front-lit, for twenty minutes,
reached out for Riddick Bowe
as momentum called me
into his crowd of hooks.

My wife will think the worst
of me. The company
I fell to once the heart bills
ate my business, too.
My printed fuckup face.
My unknown motivations.
My helmets. I bequeath them all
to avarice and selfhood,
to the body calling out,
violent and involuntary.
I lived without lights
for three retreating years.
I lived for the inward breath
accelerating, jerk of chute,
the kickback slurp of solitude
as my hand controls curled me
to the eyes of target tarps,
to a winking grey arena.
I moved to the Arctic
though I knew it meant
a place of bears.

I planned to fall on everyone:
Wembley, the '96
Inaugural, a Super Bowl.
Take cover, citizens.
I'll bombard you with no weapons,
so you can kick me where I land.
Let me eat your sins
and your competitive streaks,
your bet slips and Budweisers
and the blind smack of the surreal.

The Kodiak will claim
whatever builds a nest
in its patrol zone as its own.
I could be that lucky.
I had skills. A flair for
shock theatrics. Attendees
at the fight claimed I wept
as I descended, but it was
just the cold. The wind
at certain altitudes
will freeze your face in ecstasy.

The Quiet Man

A nest of residential Crescents:
Heathvale, Valedown, then Glenheath,
where the quiet man mows his lawn
and moves the cubes inside his brain
to sort the migrant crisis.
The city's very middle is a suburb
reabsorbed into the core.
The quiet men who live there
sort their equity and postures.

Arrière-garde domestic architecture
is overlooked by cranes, and highway signs
that East- and West- the street names.
An InfoWars sticker on a million-dollar home.
The quiet man has things to say about
your children. Nostalgia's in his nose.
A dysplasia. His apneustic nights
need a screen to smooth their worry.
Authoritarian, owner, and aglow
before his stories. When you ask
about the future it lamps imagination:
a demographic ambush. He levels his opinions
and you duck to tie your shoes.

Have enemies, friends. That's the best
that I can tell you. It is a waste to have opinions
but no enemies.
                    If a man who sits to mow his lawn
says he wishes to unleash his full potential,
stand back.

Pull your rental from its haunches
and drag it down the street.
                    It's not the people who have rage
that are a problem for this world.
It's those who have rage and comfort.

Moderately Elegiac Hat

Before Customs,
in the mirror of a nationless bathroom,
my lucky Expos tricolour
debauches business formal.
Heavy-necked, I assess the day.
I could collapse and be transported.
A man completes his declaration
and says he likes my hat. I consider myself:
caught between a thirst for silence
and soft friendship. Sealed self-regard.
Exact-change giver. Mumbleman.
My fellow traveller continues in the accent
of lilies. *How old is that?*
                    —*I've always had it.*
          It's well worn.
                    —*Thank you.*
He used to watch Rusty Staub at Jarry.
I once saw Delino DeShields
at the bistro by McGill.
We both have strike opinions.
His fingers throb unpressurized, ungloved
since the landing. We're partners now;
I adjust our hat.
                    Follow fashion for its gestures,
choose a jacket for the shrug it starts.
                    —*It's a moderately elegiac hat,* I add.
The Dyson blade swallows this thought
and so he leaves me, a smiling spirit
gone ascetic into air. Coded,
that's one more cold departure:
my rightward turn at 40, my wristwatch phase.

All these descending gadgets called to gate.
A woman takes my papers
(and compliments my shoes). The drive home
is done in comfort. Radio plays away
its script and its instructions. Sleep
and determinism rise in me two-headed.
That new treated feeling—
of being courted, of not holding court.

Triptych of the Wooden Miniatures

"Less-permanent forms like the acacia miniatures eventually come
to us only as absences indicated by their more-permanent frames,
in this case these stone display racks." —Frank Schumpeter

1. Woman

In the municipal museum's empty fourth floor,
the Egyptian miniatures reanimate their cases.
Club-headed, solemn. They're the products
of artisan committees and war. The pharaohs
didn't suffer artists. That idea came after.
A hundred nameless slaves built the miniatures,
passed word to the curators through census-path,
accounting-path. Turn, swipe your mark, stage the scene
for the night shift. Leave a joke about your master.
Doodle on his wife's unpainted breasts. But always,
flow from the dynastic lurch. Flow with appellation.
An appetite for sense. Each miniature captures
the creation of a miniature. The public space is vulgar:
you stroke the newborn earth as it forgets you.

2. Man

I'll ask the people who invent things
to stop inventing things
that make it hard to live.

Dear trickster figures, fertility gods,
keep your civil eyes on me.

The vulgar is a public space.

There is the soft concord of waking,
and then a spotlight. The morning guides the news.

Don't trust anyone over
the social imaginary.

To be broken
is to forget to love the mob.

Vulgus, mobhead, idea-bearer, rant.

To forget to be the mob
when you're alone.

3. Child

I am alive in transit.

An antlered I
repeats aloud found phrases,
phonetic feelers for the public gaze.

And given what I know of idle politics
it is best to dress myself in tees,
my son in white. To meet ourselves
in coded tones:

my King Clean Rando,
our anthemic drift.

Mob-drift. Idea-drift. Art appreciator-drift.

We have been vetted and the street has been vetted.

And a female cop
is weeping by a city tree.

Rubens's *Crucifixion*

Everybody thinks they are middle class
and handsome.

The realtor promised
a handsome modern home,
south-facing in a famous building.

The Rubens print hung
by wool around a nail,
covered a patch of water damage
left to think itself over into rot.

Head west at the door
and you're at Vienna Station.
Turn around to look upon
our brutalist ambitions.

There was no exercise room
because the homeless man who wintered there
took its parts for salvage. His middle-aged face
was handsome in his cowboy hat.

If you ask the creditors who called us
every dinnertime, my mother
was forever in the shower.

One whole decade in the shower, I told them.
She came out wrinkled.

The crucifixion follows the scene
where Christ erects his cross.
In the next scene he calls out to God.

We saw all three at the gallery
on a Free Wednesday special,
winter break of fourth grade.

I left my coat and canvas bag
inside the sculpture lobby
and had to walk home without them.

The whipping highway wind
stiffened my face.

The promise of the buildings,
handsome on the hill,
          rolled
in and out of focus with my tears.

Credo of the Security Cameras at the
St. Clair Walmart Supercentre

We believe our house brands should be raised
to see the best in people.

Our prices are prime numbers.
Our savings absolute.

That the children in our aisles aren't children.
They're temptations, tight-lidded

flasks of secret drink. Their parents twist them open
to nip from their sweet necks.

They think that we're not looking but
we are always looking.

We declare the glory of just-in-time supply chains.
The loneliness of facing.

We believe that to depreciate an asset
is to eulogize it. That the remainders

remember,

that they bear the shame of cargohood
like rescued pets. Mishandled. Chipped.

That mechanisms made by hollowed-out towns,
the migration paths of part-time work, these

are an aesthetic, and suggest
an intellect.

We don't need to know you
to find and frame your face.

Everything comes from nothing.

There were no waiting shoppers
before we set upon the off-ramp.

There was just our spot-lit sign,
the darkness it held back.

Schumpeter Tower One

To make the most of your footprint,
you can't accept stepbacks.
So the facade of the building
built before you lives on,
a heritage bear hug
around your glass prism.
Uncle to the stump of you,
which stood for the recession
until momentums returned
to make you tall and weightless.

The coffee service celebrates.
Laminates and lanyards
pocket chocolate for their mothers.
The discoverers of Davos Man
squint into the sunlight.
Their rituals are making Asia gleam.

Traffic lights switch the streets.
High and Tights and sparrow women
crane towards the lobby monitor
forever spooling stock quotes
beneath the arms of anchormen.
                The unmuted news
has called them from their cubicles.

An ambulance speeds up Adelaide
and turns onto Simcoe, pauses
like a gaze should arrive for its departure.
Like the watching is the drama it invents.

A Note on Recent Events in Our Community

We've heard a call to speak out.

We're not monsters. We at {XXXXX} are people like the weather is people. Cool wisps of content speaking common-era thought.

Our marketing manager went to Boy Scout camp and taught the boys to fish. His son is thinking about switching schools. Not because his school is bad, exactly, but because (he says:) *"like something of the fullness of the earth is missing there."*

There are fine public schools. His girlfriend goes to one. He isn't old enough to follow girls, but for him it'd be a bonus. They're only kids. Anyway, can you see how this muted public act honours a debate held inside us?

What we sell is immaterial. Our bodies are our stores of value.

My son does Scouts because I believe in service. And I worry that once unmoored from boyhood he will drift, and what if the new school brings kids who don't make good choices? It's just the two of us. We are not an enterprise of islands. We believe in tones and teamwork. Serif fonts to signify obedience to space.

We won't let you inside us, with all your concerned minds.

We hear your voice when we address ourselves. He'll be fourteen in May. We ask that you take care.

The Monster

         Did you know?
Tiananmen Square Man was not his real name.
That was the name of the photographer.
The man in the picture was only called
The Monster.
         Did you know?
It's the corner of the hour.
The June of opportunity. People,
let your default ringtones sing.

Merit is a brand. Meritocracy, a market.
I can't believe I've come this far
and made myself this patterned and impassable,
like teeth.

The Painter, 1963

"The safe was near the tail of the plane which, in one-third of a
second, was the nose of the plane as well."—Frank Schumpeter

     I don't believe in telling stories.
On descent, I only whistled.
     Pick of a late self-portrait boom,
there was only one of me,
     though I did have many brothers.
Our father had grown soft from compliments
     and the country market. I see myself, now,
from many sides at once: the nose of the plane
     is in the tail of the plane.
And I and the bodies inside both.

     You don't succumb so much
as nod to an explosive death. Incompressible blues
     respond like light in the grip of microseconds.
The diamonds, my safemates
     in the plane's warm belly,
were found by pirates riding submarines.
     Or ingested by a crab. But only I became unreal,
split and sheared by vortex forces
     and then the tidal algorithms.
My shock of shadowed hair, elbow extended
     away from the body, as if broken.
I dyed the dead in winter colours, a mist mask,
     against their skin and mandibles. Father,
I will find you
     amid these pagan afterlives and forgeries.

You who conceived me over eel stew
      and impatient lovers, a lurking American
journalist's inquests. It is natural
      for children born to aged parents
to teach themselves to grieve.

      My siblings and I were all laughed aside
by the bright new critics. Besmirched blue
      finishers' ribbons for the last rooms of every
career retrospective. One for every nation's
      ninth-best museum. But not me.
I have been encountered by the very cubist lines
      of modern physics. My threads live on
in collapsing halls of plankton.
      I alone have burst forth,
a revolution, on the earth.
I alone will live my many lives.

"The man who sold me the eggs stepped to the gates one morning at the Uxbridge house. A quiet man, polite. He brought with him a mirror and a small girl he said was his daughter. We made them lunch. The eggs in a green canvas bag.

The same with the woman who sold the Kandinsky screenprints. A mirror and a little girl. Canvas bags.

The Emin tent, too—do you not believe me? Okay, don't believe me.

Everyone who comes here wants to hear a story just to interrupt its telling. They ask me for answers, and then pull the words down." —Frank Schumpeter, 2016

Alta Vista

Frank,
your mother loved you. Your *oma* combed your hair.
Your invented city set its mind
to immobile matters. This made you firm and passionate.
Man of means: when the high school hockey team
leaves the locker room for home ice,
they tap your nameplate for good luck. Like you,
I had myself three goals: to not be baffled by the world,
to shape a family in the tall grass,
and to find wonder where it shows itself.
Do these seem abstract to you? I'd bet.

Did you know I watched you die? Frank,
I found the room at the far end of your first named wing,
where the hospital looked upon your Innovation Courtyard.
I was there for a drama too intimate to tell you.
I pushed through your thicket of gift shop roses,
spotted the Fabergé eggs
the gallery desired. Nine or ten grey men,
hunched shoulders and good suits.
I heard your house in Durham went to market
the day you first got sick. The Tampa condo dimmed its lights.
Your only daughter cancelled on her sponsor
and fell into a California King full of terriers.

To be loved and of the world is ecstatic,
and an example for men whose goals are all adages.
I watched your contented belly breathe until
the grey men noticed me and shouldered dark the window.
I don't remember what killed you. Was it all the art?

Is it class betrayal to be curious? Frank,
I don't make much money,
though I am shallow and destructive like you were.

I promise I don't count you as a father,
though I was raised beneath your roof.
My real father lies dying, dimmed and one-legged,
in a government room. The tabloids declared you
their favourite son. The CBC caught flack
when an architecture critic spoke his feelings.
I never said I saw you—Frank, Franz, father—
I kept it to myself. When the eggs went up
in your Lost Things Wing, its new protectors wept.
When I said that we're both shallow and destructive,
Frank,
            I meant we made our lives
            out of found materials.
We stuck our names on the parts
where the shame might leak and claim us.

"Giant Hot Air Balloon of Vincent van Gogh's Head Fails to Launch in Toronto"

All of our news can be traced to the glaciers.
Wit, water, lake effects, an impulse
to look east or south for culture.

Come to the lakeshore
and see them lift a ginger suicide
high into the sky.

He will not cooperate.

On foot the night before,
heat warnings grumbling my pocket,
I thought about stubbornness and dying alone.

The newspaper office is converting to condos,
but the condos need to serve a short sentence
as gallery space before this.

Their infinity room is lined with pipes.
Spotlights shift from farm to city, darken
for handwritten elegies and madness traps.

The paintings dance among us,
we who paid to sit in marked circles
and watch them spin and segue.

I witness *Wheatfield with Crows*
projected in my wife's hair,
irises drawn along her skin.

Farmhouse in Provence
is sucked out the exit.
Guards alert the napping.

The gift shop: Vincent's head
and ear are sold separately.

I buy a kaleidoscope
and stand within it
for my son's fine attentions.

In the summer light
the lake waves
rotate around their axes.

He is watching me
watch the workers
try to raise their head again.

Man at the Crossroads Looking with Uncertainty but with Hope
and High Vision to the Choosing of a New and Better Future

Picasso and Matisse said no,
so Mother settled on the shaggy
Mexican muralist in Detroit.
She found a sketchbook he had made
                              (I was told) in Russia.
Took it to the office for opinions.
We paid him double, as New York is two Detroits.

We wanted our lobby to woo everyone:
worker, craftsman, lady-worker, capital.
Then beam them back home until they found themselves
curled in their very own transformers. It's radio,
it requires big ideas.
                    An eager symbolism
linking each figure to a policy polling
10–20% among the national electorate.
An entire secret alphabet of fringe.

The pipes he placed beneath the figures carried meaning.
The workers' uniforms were
                              (I was told) all denim.
The cells in his microscope were,
                              (I was told) syphilitic.
I spotted Lenin in a corner, gladhanding sharecroppers.
A hammer and a sickle in the washing light of stars.
My father called the architect, an insurance firm, his wife.
The opening was scheduled,
                              (I was told) for May 1st.

But by April we had veiled it in burlap.
Celebrated that summer with Dubonnet and chisels.
Then a head-down walk to feed the mob.

Triptych for Gustav Klimt at the University of Vienna

"If you'll allow a more dramatic reading, their very existence was a fire." —Frank Schumpeter

1. Philosophy

To go unloved your whole life is like this:
>   an acoustic dark, bedsores on the mirror.
>   The critics and the censors are cousins,
>   sorting machines dropped like jaws
>   between a benevolent idea and its art.

To paint on a ceiling is like this:
>   you are always frowning at the gods.
>   The constant someones who blot out clouds
>   are cornering your enemies.
>   Are holding a tarp over your progress.

To not outlive a war is like this:
>   all your music holds its final notes.
>   The edges of your canvases fold inward
>   as if making to ship themselves home.
>   As if shamed to shyness by their nudes.

To die by a fire is like this:
>   you curve your taut arms until
>   your eye sockets swallow up your fists
>   and the body spills into ablutions,
>   makes itself a fountain in the square.

2. Medicine

The men who yelled
Pornography! like
the word lived,

wriggling,
inside their hot mouths—
they had no politics.

They just happened
to hate you
and owned an institution.

Take heart.
Take the compliment.
The compliment is art.

O,

little witch-house.
Wit house.
With us always.

Name your lost forsaken
and we'll march
upon its grave.

3. Jurisprudence

But why would there need to be more than one god of vengeance?
These three are all sleeping, or distracted.

The building is on fire,
but not the roof.

The roof looks over its shoulder
to the two retreating armies,
suns its holy ass on the war.

Nostalgia Man Rises

We waded in the desert, or programmed our remotes.
We ate our spiceless food and shopped for culture.

Whole portfolios of firms competed for our childhoods.
Figurines emerged and were exoticized for depth.

Now even cop shows explain themselves in superhero code.
The monomyth groans for the lonely. I can't fault

these serial blinders. Franchises give order. There
are real terrors and they are hard to manage.

This all happened before you were born,
before the origin stories ate the bones of all narrative.

One summer in the '80s, every month
brought a new small boy with a robot.

Their dads were scared of scarcity and Russia.
I am scared of pulpits and momentum. And scarcity and Russia.

I have the tone of a movie that used to be a book.
I am a scene in which everyone is running

into a sabotage of genre. Themes and credits
have been pushed to my perimeter.

My lessons
are so small and episodic.

Stands For
for O

The A word is *avarice*. The B word is *bitch*, which
you picked up one perfect Tuesday after school,
were made to cleanse to its initial.
It follows that the C word is *comportment*
and the D word is *defer*. The E word
is *earn*, its trod towards routine
and its transactions. The F word is *forever*.
The G word is *grammar*. The H word *(hesitate)*
comes from the language of my father, where it means:
"to hold a stammer so long it becomes punctuation."
The I word is *I*.
The J word is my name.
The K word comes along once a generation,
is a misspelling of a common word for family.
The L word, *luxuriate*, happens in the mind.
The M and N words are *moderate* and *nation*.
O, a sound to remind the body of desire, gives us *only*.
The P word is *parrot*. The Q word, *quest*.
The R and S words are cousins: *reassure* and *savour*.
Both of whom run their dry tongues over wisdom
but are truthfully ways we relax into the known.
The T word is *temper*. The U word is *unsaid*.

> Like how I'd never say
> that this exercise is coverage,
> a gesture via negatives
> to a world-sense that's edgeless,
> a land that can't be mapped.

The V word is *violence*, which you pronounce: *violins*.
You also pronounce my name as *just-enoughness*
and the family as *king*.

The W word is the U word twice.
The X word is the plus sign.
The Y word is *Yes*.
The Z word scans for stalwarts
like a bird inside a cage. Stay quiet, *zealotry*,
I'll come for you by morning.

Alias Jimmy Valentine

"The last of three adaptations of the play in a fifteen-year span . . . four reels remain, along with pieces of the hastily added soundtrack." —Frank Schumpeter

Place your ear against the safe to hear your old life as an archetype.

~

There is no lost sound to the machine.

~

Jimmy is the common stock of touring companies. A silence picture.

~

He has cold motives.

~

Word of sound came down as they packaged up the reels.

~

They went back to the studio and spoke into the gaps.

~

They. The *they* there are Barrymore and foley boys.

~

There was no such thing as foley boys.

~

They went back to the studio and invented themselves.

~

Barrymore was also a composer and an artist.

~

To play his songs beneath his drawings could be called *A Photoplay*.

~

The human ear is shaped to wrap around a lock.

~

What if Barrymore pulled the film to paint in a talkie's drum?

~

What if his voice didn't transfer?

~

What if the last line in the picture was: *Go to Little Rock, Jimmy. I never go to Little Rock.*

~

And then Jimmy looked straight into the camera?

Three-Mile Panorama of the Mississippi River

I'll draw you in, American-eyed pedestrians of London.
Keep your minds aloft, your nose out of the mud
and my misshapen fauna. I'm self-taught. Take an arm,
and make your long blue way down the delta,
through the valley laid out like paid imagination
around the castle grounds. I don't owe you more
than what magic makes between us. A cut-up canvas
in a farmer's shed in Lexington. One in Charleston.
One draped around a lady from Edinburgh
who wore it to her grave, cape of switchgrass
tucked over Scottish shoulders. Walk with a lover.
I know lovers like admission prices: they're fluid.

Musicians visible in certain light
between the sun and stitching scars
play the best *Yankee Doodle Dandy*
local studio hands could slap together. Fix your gaze,
the couples up ahead are rivercraft.
Stubbornness, slave narratives
and the pop of new concessions
return to their motherland like men hit by lightning:
wide-eyed, buckled at their knees.
                              Notice nothing.
My three-mile panorama is just 3,000 feet.
Whose feet, yours? They could be.

I funded this work by selling minor landscapes
and helping hunters clean their kill.
They'll have it disassembled into pieces for the trip.
Restored in Maine and struck for Boston. Put up,
cut down. One last time and then
left for cloth and burping blankets. A doll's dress.
Teepees hanging in a child's room.
Somewhere in the Reconstruction South
there's a painting of a bearded northerner,
easel underarm. That's me.
I drew myself in, one tourist for another.
I will always be where I take you.

The Queen Assiniboine

I was your art and on your money.

Make me, colonial cheerleaders for credit and for Canada,
        make me mourned and solemn,
like the portraits hung on schoolchildren.

Snake River, Red River, Assiniboine:
        you plaid-hearted tributary folk
will know my state frown for its face of calm reserve.

The banking system only suffers when the runs come in waves.
        My crown collects itself, taxes the heart
and my headwaters

with a clear and bug-eyed bust. I'm an island now,
        sunk to my cheeks in the southbound flow of silt
on its standard way

to commerce and the border. I have two sisters,
        Queens Merseyside and Leeds still sit atop their thrones
safe from English water.

The sculptor shipped me off to idle Winnipeg
        where I overlooked Assiniboine.
But I can overlook more.

My eyes are granite, I could see clear across the city
        to Academy Road, Saint Boniface. But lately
I've been looking at my hands.

I will overlook the sun if you lay me down face up.
    I will overlook my sun
if you lay me in my river.

"The Coyote Is Always More Humiliated than Harmed by His Failures"

If I didn't plan for dinner, my directness
would introduce nothing but my self-defeat.
I ask the moustache-twirler wound inside of me
to plate a silent prayer for mangy boys
and ridicule. Don't look at me, I'm eating.

One year, the lights dimmed on peak expression
and I began to slap myself to show frustration.
Cartoon-like at lower speeds, antic at fast ones.
It was not a punishment raised against my own person,
but control bloating out into encounter.

I lampooned until my ribs accordioned
with synchrony and sound effects. Saying:
I'm in pain, and I am pain's performer.
The ache I raise is made to be displayed.

For Jeremy

"... anxiety is a Jewish import. No one knew it in the Christian West until they took it over. You feel like that when you don't have a culture." —Comment in the Facebook group Weird Toronto, 2019

In your picture, a blond kid in a purple shirt
stands beneath a willow tree. I made out an arrow
and the embossed word *Catholic*.
First I searched: *neonazi archery clubs, Toronto*.

Then local Catholic high schools and spotted
the purple St. Paul's Archers. Your last name
brought a woman's LinkedIn headshot, partner
in a downtown firm and founder of the *St. Paul's*

Parents' Committee. Her public Facebook
gave eight pages of vacation. Some tagged
a younger you, attached to an old account
that liked a bunch of early edgelord stuff

then was left for the motherless one last year.
As a pre-teen, Jeremy, you smiled from your molars
and believed in the Leafs. Your mom launched a petition
against the redistricting of two junior schools.

I queried the redistricting. It bussed a stretch
of Lonsdale Avenue uptown to St. Augustine's.
I looked for you on Lonsdale. Nothing, but a man
who also shares your surname was interviewed eight years ago

about a fire that took down a Victorian gem two blocks
from Grace Church. He's not connected to your mother
but I found him in your contacts. Current city: Markham.
Did Mom keep her married name to stop her clients wondering?

Dad said he woke to flames across the street.
The story gave the fire at 383 Lonsdale. Google Maps
shows a gawky McMansion now.
Reset the date to see the empty lot.

Across the road is 382. A willow tree halos the yard.
I printed the comment and stuck your school's address
as return, left it at my office with reception.

Dear Jeremy,

Don't be frightened. I wanted to reach out
coolly from the abstract to announce myself
as reader. When I tell people about you,
I'll disguise your data and provide a new name.

Jeremy is both the one good Pearl Jam single
and the name of my friend who drank too much
and froze to death passed out in a snowbank
in Banff at nineteen. I don't wish for you to freeze to death,

Jeremy, though, people say it's peaceful.
I just wanted to share
this one thing about myself
for the five or six I know about you.

[This video has been removed by request of the victims' families]

The body will become a siren.
Your own body, and others.

Given space, a shooter will cell-split,
will ululate to unknown partners,

collide with the upturned faces
of commuters. Not knowing

is our core condition. Sense beckons,
buzzes in the blur of pirated footage,

a breeze in the garden of crowds. This
is paradise. There are unconfirmed reports

and then there is comfort. Photo tricks
and fibs. There's a contextual itch

for the act to form a story. The light's resolve
on suspect skin is your isolated politics.

It flickers from its unexamined space like an exit.
Make the face that says you're not surprised.

Daytime weathermen and kid videographers
click in on scenes-in-progress, become the root language

of every other speech. Become source.
Cameras are or aren't our lizard instincts,

linger-headed drones of lust or curiosity.
Someone is a doctor. Someone says he went north,

and whole machines turn their trumpet bells
to blast him into networks.

Avatars are plucked from hurried pixels
and stretched the world over,

they merge into profiles
whose owners wake to push notifications

that say they'll soon be punished.
Breathless is the call to come witness.

Opinion captions lie on looping video. Watch:
an unidentified figure steps out from the crowd

and raises his one known arm. Follow him.
The future is wherever he is pointing.

Triptych for the House of Fabergé

"In 1917, when the revolution breached the palace, all the eggs could do was call attention to themselves." —Frank Schumpeter

1. Hen with Sapphire Pendant

There is something I would like to represent to you,
the People. My stump-speech comeuppance.
　　　　My familial skin, which flinches when caressed
by loving fire. Let go of this luxuriating core
　　　　of ore-covered egg, with its sediment scraped
off imperial furs. Its empire style. I am not
　　　　the historical footnote certain captains of anarchy
commanded me to be. I glow and burn their pamphlets.
　　　　Know me as stained glass. A riot-bred, intemperate,
art-eating vessel. I am the classless
　　　　mother-fodder of the mob, head of my brood
made of Fabergé genetics. Sing my revolution.
　　　　Print me in the papers for the soldiers who can't read.

2. Maria's Mauve

       Maria made her hands-across-Europe yoke
to seed the czar a peaceful generation.
       She made her home St. Petersburg,
made love like a bearskin folded on a rack,
       but still a wild flicker from the fire in her eye.
Etiquette levels the lip in times of crisis,
       guards against the guillotine blades
that fall like rain. Heave your gift
       onto its surprise made of mining rights and duty,
onto the bespoke souls of nobles.
       Happy Easter, Russia. Here are your dead children.
You are not the knowing grin
       that shoulders all your appetite. Hold yourself,
show the smoke but live within the flash.

3. *The Alexander III*

Who's a bad boy? Empire is a bad boy.
Who devoured Russia? Runt of the litter
  devoured Russia. Runt of Russian history.
If you have Oedipal issues, let me tell you:
  that avuncular ointment, cure carried east,
that severance of namesake, I know it more
  than anyone. I have been on all the journeys
from the ballroom to the banquet hall.
  So send the Winter Palace, I'll reflect her from her mantle.
Send the winter egg. I'll raise my good doomed children.
  What is Russia but a cap to keep Europe
from escaping? O Mother, I don't know
  what was meant for me except to sit for paintings,
and find myself betrothed to lovely cousins.

The bearded men of the boat's lit half
and the bearded men of its dark half
do not agree on anything. Anger arrives,
first as metaphor, then farce.
Associate yourself with aft answers.
                                        Jesus,
or someone with a nose just like his,
palpitates a heart in Hero's Row.
Make a statement about strong spines
and sticktoitiveness
and home. Say what you will
about the Prosperity Gospel,
at least those people
believed in close readings.
                        Not you,
your legs are too swollen.
Your back shrieks Amber Alerts
when throwing out the trash.
Come, harvest copper wire
from the walls inside your youth.
You beetroot-sucking,
lumpenproletariat display,
don't be the cliché
made for others making points.
You don't know what you're doing,
dummy. You're talking to the waves.

von Neumann's Unfinished

"*The Computer and the Brain* was eventually brought together from speeches and notes, and published with a dust jacket that showed von Neumann smiling in front of the Institute's computer. By the time of the photo, his work on the Hydrogen Bomb was complete and he had converted to Catholicism." —Frank Schumpeter

Onward, solace hole.
A moustachioed man and I are reading our non-fictions.

Our sleep-deprived descent into granite tubes
that squeal south to the city centre.

I can see his marginalia and his nose hairs.
Together, we explore the twenty-first century.

Our businesswear is showing
through the slips in winter jackets.

Laptops not respecting public norms
flaunt movie rips and GitHub.

Peripheral devices
suckle at my ears.

The moustachioed man lifts an eye of recognition
over von Neumann's final sanity, meets my own

as if to say *Hello,* but to the book.
I would hate von Neumann

and he would hate me.
But the man does not hate me,

in this reticulated life
where he is not von Neumann

(who did not confess his sins),
and I am not the man I seem to be.

Triptych: Theories of the Adaptation

1. Ogden Nash: The Wizard of Oz

That the text is a set. A single sonic effort.
That the production is encoded
with the names of its characters
and the names of the actors
who will come to play those characters,
all inferred from title sheets.
That there is no work except
that first creative heave, and so
when they said to write a script
you showed up with four soft pages.

They inquired why
so you telegraphed a gesture,
took the clock off the wall
to watch its wound hands twitch.
When the men who owned the rights
frowned at one another,
you caught their fallen dander
as it drifted to their ashtrays.

You set the dander up
with plans and motivations.
Posed it for piano track,
let it explore those motivations
on their brown boardroom table,
                      lit red
by a single cherry spotlight
                 loaned
from the shoot across the street.

2. *Aldous Huxley: Alice in Wonderland*

You will sit in hot rooms
and they will bring you bits of script to make more British.
You'll impart what you know about the Regency era.

But the Carroll screenplay is yours from the book.
Except when a factotum taps you on the shoulder
to say the rabbit should have spectacles.

An adaptation reenacts the writing of its source.
A splash of language and a bibliography,
then jokes spread over final pages like jam.

You'll quit before they clobber you with meetings.
Disney said he barely understood a third of it.
Luckily it's three times longer than required.

Leaving, you'll cross the lot to find a woman selling cigarettes.
You'll tell her the story of the story as you know it.
She'll smile at you gamely. She wants to be an actress.

Years later, you'll sit in a cinema in Inglewood,
laugh at the bit about the cat. The company kept your notes
but never once used them. The boss says they never got it right.

3. James Lineberger: T*A*P*S

James, are you alive? I need you.
The *Collected* you had printed was lost in the rain
and I can't remember your address or advice.

You schlepped a wrathful second act to Cincinnati.
Your stubborn Story credit haunting IMDb.
Single-shot Hollywood deserter,
scion of a decade's brood brigade, imaginer
of Cruise and Penn's first lines. I picture you
in community theatre, coaxing teen soliloquies
so incredibly fast we cannot say
who or what we are until the film glides through
and what comes after that last bit, James?

I miss your long sad poems
about elder abuse and marriage.

What comes next after coming home
if it's not the object lesson of your life,
escorted by ambition through its frame?

Comparing Rivers I Have Never Visited to the Don

The elongated Don. The dammed Don.

The Don that,
until the construction of the Gorky Reservoir,
flowed into the Volga at Kostroma. The eponymous Don.

An unnamed minor Don. The Don herself.

The Don on fire in your photograph.
The Don your father dropped his fingers into
as the sun crept towards a full eclipse.

The Don of cypress trees.
The Don of Cyprus.

The Don that home runs settle in. The rounded Don.

The Don that is not one Don but rather
a hundred small tributaries
assembling like ants at the mouth of the Atlantic.

The disrupted Don. The Don of Chinese industry.

The implacable Don. Sister Dons.

The Don that grew so fetid it was buried by decree.
The Don that does not see you coming.

Don of Simcoe County. Don of cowards.

Fairweather Don. Miracle Don.

Don devouring its banks. The Don which,
science says, will dry up and spill a million refugees next summer.

The seismographer's Don, elliptical Don,
Precambrian Don, hot Don.

Don of a neighbouring planet.
The Don, abstracted.

A longer Don. End Don.

Damned Don.
The Don I will deliver you.

The next Don, your Don.

      The Don
that you are writing from.

Your retreating
tidal Don.

Schumpeter Park

—overnight,
the plaques light up.

A man in a baseball cap
wipes down the caution tape.

Another man refreshes
the sponsoring brands.

I like to park the car.
I like to take long walks.

There is no one to say hi to,
but they'd know me all by sight.

I pretend to walk a dog.
I hold my arm ahead of me.

Frank's Wing, its glass stairs,
dissolve into our sky.

We are not afraid of applications
to address the civic worry.

We're afraid of open spaces
overlooked by open roofs.

Everyone I Have Ever Slept with 1963–1995

The problem with love poems
is they were all secretly written
by the government.

Why would I take a picture?
We will be like this again.

And I will see us then,
friend. I will see us then.

Alta Vista

I'm worried you might read this first,
and that would be a kind of nudity. A show of cards
and source deceptions. Joseph Schumpeter had only one child.

Joseph Jr. and his mother both died from his birth.
He lived a single Friday, then passed inside his mourning blanket.
The text imagines, in the fictional Franz ("Frank") Schumpeter,

Annie's survival and a second shot at family. The Schumpeter
 Wing
is modelled after the Art Gallery of Ontario's South Gallery,
built in 2008 by Toronto hero Frank Gehry.

Schumpeter Park is Grange Park, a public space reopened
in 2017, bordered by the South Gallery
and the Ontario College of Art and Design University.

Frank's highway is the Spadina Expressway,
a proposed route into downtown Toronto,
begun in the 1960s before

being struck down by protest. As designed,
it was to cut through the Cedarvale Ravine
and end at the corner of Bloor St. and Spadina Rd.

Alta Vista Tower is derived from The Vincennes,
a building built in 1966 by the architect Uno Prii,
one hundred metres from Bloor and Spadina.

I lived in The Vincennes with my own young family
from 2015 to 2019, before being renovicted
by its current owners, Starlight Investments.

If anyone from Starlight Investments
is reading this:
fuck you.

The model for Schumpeter Tower One
is the Bay Adelaide Centre at 333 Bay.
Joseph Schumpeter did not originate the term

"creative destruction."
It was first coined by Werner Sombart,
who borrowed it from Marx.

Also: the Dionne Brand quote in Grange Park
is from *Thirsty* (2002); the Kandinsky quote
is from a 1916 letter to Gabrielle Münter;

Schumpeter's Harry Shearer story comes from a 1992 issue
of *Spy* magazine; the James Lineberger excerpt
is from "Words, These Soft Words" (2008);

Frank's epigraph to "*The Painter*, 1963"
quotes Stephen Kimber
in Aly Thomson's 2018 article for the Canadian Press;

"Giant Hot Air Balloon of Vincent van Gogh's Head
Fails to Launch in Toronto" is the title of a 2021 article
for blogTO by Lauren O'Neil; and

"The Coyote Is Always More Humiliated than Harmed by His
    Failures"
is the ninth of Chuck Jones's "Nine Unbreakable Rules for
Encounters between Wile E. Coyote and the Road Runner."

Thanks to the Canada Council
and the Toronto Arts Council
for sending blessed cheques.

Thanks to the press—Michael, Emily,
and the people who think all day
about books.

The Reconstruction Efforts are ekphrastic poems
(poems responding to works of art)
with the complexifier that these *ghost ekphrastics*

are from works that I've never seen,
and cannot expect to see,
as they are lost, destroyed, or were ephemeral.

Certain ghost ekphrastics owe a debt to the Tate Museum's
online exhibition The Gallery of Lost Art
and the accompanying book *Lost Art* by Jennifer Mundy.

Despite collector's efforts, my relationship with most art
living or lost
is the same as yours: I will pass it by.

Thank you to the magazines who printed these poems.
Thanks to readers: Adam, Adèle, Alexis, Cassidy, George,
Hollay, Matt, and Paul. The whole book is for Lex.

Streaming services say the top songs I listened to
in the years I spent here were "Oldie," "Good News,"
and "The Light of a Clear Blue Morning."

Lastly, the kid in the Disneyland poem
will be forty this summer.
This means that we both made it.

ELYSE FRIEDMAN

Jacob McArthur Mooney's previous collections have been shortlisted for the Trillium Book Award in Poetry and the Dylan Thomas Prize. Originally from Nova Scotia, he now lives in Toronto with his family. *Frank's Wing* is his fourth book.

This book is also available as a Global Certified Accessible™ (GCA) ebook. ECW Press's ebooks are screen reader friendly and are built to meet the needs of those who are unable to read standard print due to blindness, low vision, dyslexia, or a physical disability.

At ECW Press, we want you to enjoy our books in whatever format you like. If you've bought a print copy just send an email to ebook@ecwpress.com and include:

- the book title
- the name of the store where you purchased it
- a screenshot or picture of your order/receipt number and your name
- your preference of file type: PDF (for desktop reading), ePub (for a phone/tablet, Kobo, or Nook), mobi (for Kindle)

A real person will respond to your email with your ebook attached. Please note this offer is only for copies bought for personal use and does not apply to school or library copies.

Thank you for supporting an independently owned Canadian publisher with your purchase!